LGBTQ AT WORK

YOUR PERSONAL AND WORKING LIFE

Beyond Male and Female: The Gender Identity Spectrum

Body and Mind: LGBTQ Health Issues

Double Challenge: Being LGBTQ and a Minority

Gender Fulfilled: Being Transgender

LGBTQ Without Borders: International Life

LGBTQ at Work: Your Personal and Working Life

Love Makes a Family: Friends, Family, and Significant Others

When You're Ready: Coming Out

You Are Not Alone: Finding Your LGBTQ Community

LGBTQ AT WORK

YOUR PERSONAL AND WORKING LIFE

By Melissa Albright-Jenkins

Mason Crest
Philadelphia • Miami

Mason Crest
450 Parkway Drive, Suite D
Broomall, PA 19008
(866) MCP-BOOK (toll free)
www.masoncrest.com

Printed in the United States of America
First printing
9 8 7 6 5 4 3 2 1
Series ISBN: 978-1-4222-4273-5
Hardcover ISBN: 978-1-4222-4278-0
E-book ISBN: 978-1-4222-7525-2

Cataloging-in-Publication Data is available on file at the Library of Congress.

Developed and Produced by Print Matters Productions, Inc. (www.printmattersinc.com)

Cover and Interior Design by Tim Palin Creative

QR CODES AND LINKS TO THIRD-PARTY CONTENT

CONTENTS

KEY ICONS TO LOOK FOR

WORDS TO UNDERSTAND: These words, with their easy-to-understand definitions, will increase readers' understanding of the text, while building vocabulary skills.

SIDEBARS: This boxed material within the main text allows readers to build knowledge, gain insights, explore possibilities, and broaden their perspectives by weaving together additional information to provide realistic and holistic perspectives.

EDUCATIONAL VIDEOS: Readers can view videos by scanning our QR codes, providing them with additional educational content to supplement the text.

TEXT-DEPENDENT QUESTIONS: These questions send the reader back to the text for more careful attention to the evidence presented there.

RESEARCH PROJECTS: Readers are pointed toward areas of further inquiry connected to each chapter. Suggestions are provided for projects that encourage deeper research and analysis.

SERIES GLOSSARY OF KEY TERMS: This back-of-the-book glossary contains terminology used throughout this series. Words found here increase the reader's ability to read and comprehend higher-level books and articles in this field.

Foreword

I'm so excited that you've decided to pick up this book! I can't tell you how much something like this would have meant to me when I was in high school in the early 2000s. Thinking back on that time, I can honestly say I don't recall ever reading anything positive about the LGBTQ community. And while *Will & Grace* was one of the most popular shows on television at the time, it never made me feel as though such stories could be a reality for me. That's in part why it took me nearly a decade more to finally come out in 2012 when I was 25 years old; I guess I knew so little about what it meant to be LGBTQ that I was never really able to come to terms with the fact that I was queer myself.

But times have changed so much since then. In the United States alone, marriage equality is now the law of the land; conversion therapy has been banned in more than 15 states (and counting!); all 50 states have been served by an openly LGBTQ-elected politician in some capacity at some time; and more LGBTQ artists and stories are being celebrated in music, film, and on television than ever before. And that's just the beginning! It's simply undeniable: *it gets better.*

After coming out and becoming the proud queer person I am today, I've made it my life's goal to help share information that lets others know that they're never alone. That's why I now work for the It Gets Better Project (www.itgetsbetter.org), a nonprofit with a mission to uplift, empower, and connect LGBTQ youth around the globe. The organization was founded in September 2010 when the first It Gets Better video was uploaded to YouTube. The viral online storytelling movement that quickly followed has generated over 60,000 video stories to date, one of the largest collections of LGBTQ stories the world has ever seen.

Since then, the It Gets Better Project has expanded into a global organization, working to tell stories and build communities everywhere. It does this through three core programs:

- **Media.** We continue to expand our story collection to reflect the vast diversity of the global LGBTQ community and to make it ever more accessible to LGBTQ youth everywhere. (See, itgetsbetter.org/stories.)
- **Global.** Through a growing network of affiliates, the It Gets Better Project is helping to equip communities with the knowledge, skills, and resources they need to tell their own stories. (See, itgetsbetter.org/global.)
- **Education.** It Gets Better stories have the power to inform our communities and inspire LGBTQ allies, which is why we're working to share them in as many classrooms and community spaces we can. (See, itgetsbetter.org/education.)

You can help the It Gets Better Project make a difference in the lives of LGBTQ young people everywhere. To get started, go to www.itgetsbetter.org and click "Get Involved." You can also help by sharing this book and the other incredible volumes from the LGBTQ Life series with someone you know and care about. You can also share them with a teacher or community leader, who will in turn share them with countless others. That's how movements get started.

In short, I'm so proud to play a role in helping to bring such an important collection like this to someone like you. I hope you enjoy each and every book, and please don't forget: *it gets better.*

Justin Tindall
Director, Education and
Global Programming
It Gets Better Project

Introduction

As an LGBTQ individual, navigating the professional work environment can be tricky. If you are working in an area that is conservative, or you fear retaliation if people find out you are not straight, working in a new company can be a daunting experience. When you stay true to who you are, develop strong personal boundaries, and learn how to use social media responsibly, you should be able to live your life as you choose to, without fear of being fired for who you are. Unfortunately, for people living in half of the states, you can still be fired for being gay.

There's no reason you are obligated to come out at work, and for many people, keeping their LGBTQ status private is the answer. While you aren't ashamed of who you are, this doesn't mean you have to share your personal life with anyone. You don't have to come out, but in certain situations you may feel comfortable sharing your LGBTQ status. In states where the rights of LGBTQ people are protected, it may be much easier for you to feel confident in coming out to coworkers. Coming out at work is a personal decision and one that you can make when the time is right.

Social media are great ways to see what your friends and family are up to, but they are also mine fields for those who are trying to keep their LGBTQ status private. Pay attention to your privacy settings, knowing that you don't have to friend everyone who wants to be your friend on social media. Learn what your company has for a social media policy. It is always best to avoid friending anyone from your work environment until you find out what your company's exact policy is.

Some companies don't allow supervisors to be friends on social media with the people they supervise. In general, this is a good rule of thumb to follow. When you supervise people, you don't want them to have access to your personal life through social media, even if your company allows it. You spend a lot of time with people at work, and social media should be used to relax and enjoy your time away from work.

If you are asked why you won't become friends with coworkers on social media, you can state that you don't really use them much. If it is an individual you supervise, simply state that being friends on social media is not allowed. There are rules in most companies regarding social media use, and it is your job to know what the rules are.

When you are in a committed domestic partnership or married to your same-sex partner, your partner may be entitled to receive benefits such as health insurance from your new job. While it might make you nervous about setting up benefits for your same-sex partner, understand that the human resources department must keep any information you share about your private life confidential.

As an employee in any company, there may be times when you come across insensitive people. You may feel as though the environment is harsh or even dangerous for those who are LGBTQ. If you come across people who are homophobic, you don't have to handle them on your own. You can talk to your supervisor or take your concerns to the human resources department. You have the right to feel safe at work, and you should speak to your immediate supervisor first if you feel uncomfortable.

Discrimination happens for many reasons. People can be discriminated against because of their sexual identity, age, skin color, and more. It isn't always easy to prove discrimination, but it occurs in many forms for a wide range of people. If you feel that you are

THE RISE OF SOCIAL MEDIA

Social media began around 1999, when blogging started and became popular among users. Facebook was developed in 2004 and quickly became the most widely used social media network available, gaining ground of a similar profile-sharing site called MySpace. Facebook is the number one social media network used among those over 30 years old, while other sites such as Instagram and Snapchat are more popular among younger social media users. Employers have had to develop social media policies to address the use and friendship development between employees, those they supervise, and clients.

overlooked for a promotion because of your LGBTQ status, take the time to talk to your supervisor about what you could improve to get the promotion next time. It may be that you aren't ready for a promotion, and you were quick to judge that it was because of your LGBTQ status.

When you are true to yourself and you take the time to learn about what you want to do for work, you are more likely to find a job that you love. If the environment doesn't feel comfortable, try to promote a more positive work environment. Look for ways to include others in discussions, and don't be afraid to stand up for someone people are talking about negatively.

As you learn about work and personal life balance, you will discover what it means to have boundaries. You can share some personal information without telling everyone all the details of your private life. The more you are able to keep your personal and private life separate, the easier it will be for you to live your life in both areas.

Professional boundaries are going to make it easier for you to build healthy work relationships, while being able to focus on your work. People who get too intimate at work tend to discuss too much personal information at work, while leaving their job duties neglected.

As an LGBTQ person, you will benefit from building relationships that work for you and don't involve sharing information on social media. Learn how to have boundaries, and don't be afraid to speak up when you feel it is necessary.

Establishing professional boundaries will make it easier to focus on your work.

1

Coming Out in the Workplace

WORDS TO UNDERSTAND

COMING OUT: Coming out of the closet, *or simply* coming out, *is a metaphor for LGBT people's self-disclosure of their sexual orientation or of their gender identity.*

DISCRIMINATION: *The unjust or prejudicial treatment of different categories of people or things, especially on the grounds of race, age, or sex.*

TRANSGENDER: *Denoting or relating to a person whose senses of personal identity and gender do not correspond with their birth sex.*

Coming out at work is a personal decision. When you identify as LGBTQ, letting your colleagues and coworkers know may feel like a priority. But you have the right to share your personal information when you are ready, and not before. Be patient. Coming out in the workplace can take time, and you can go slowly by getting to know people and finding those you connect with and can trust.

When you have a new job, your skills and talents are what matter most. If you feel comfortable sharing your status as an LGBTQ individual, consider the setting where you want to disclose this information. For example, do you mention in front of a colleague in the break room that you are **transgender**? Do you share in a meeting? Knowing when to share the information is as important as whether to share and can help you feel more comfortable in your place of work.

CONSIDER YOUR MOTIVES

Motives matter when it comes to coming out at work. If you are newly identified as an LGBTQ individual, you may feel as though it's important to tell every single person you come in contact with. But before you do, it's important to ask yourself why you feel the need to

It's natural to want to tell every single person you come in contact with when you first come out.

Try normalizing the conversation by stating your relationship as a fact.

share this information. Are you proud of your status and trying to make a bold statement at work? Do you want your co-workers to know because you don't want to hide who you are? Do you fear **discrimination** and want to clearly identify your status so that others understand your concern?

Whatever your motives may be, there are better and worse ways to share your LGBTQ status. In most cases, you don't have to make a bold statement. For example, in casual conversation you could mention your boyfriend or girlfriend, wife or husband. Try

The more comfortable you are being yourself, the easier it is for people to accept you.

normalizing the conversation by stating your relationship as fact without feeling as though you have to explain yourself. In situations where you aren't comfortable, feel free to use gender-neutral language, such as *partner* or *spouse*, to avoid any unnecessary conversations you don't want to have.

BE YOURSELF

The world is changing. It was once much harder, if not downright dangerous, for LGBTQ individuals to come out at work. You may encounter situations at work where you do not want to share personal information, but generally, the more comfortable you are

Find a mentor who can help you navigate how you present yourself to the world.

simply being yourself, the easier it will be for others to accept who you are. When you are true to yourself, it will be easier to be who you are, no matter what. You don't have to think about your life as a political statement.

FIND PROFESSIONAL SUPPORT

If you are newly identifying as LGBTQ, find some professional support or a mentor who can help you navigate how you present yourself to the world. You may feel as though everyone is judging you, or that everyone can tell about your new identity just by looking at you, but remember, most people simply aren't paying that close attention.

One excellent source of professional support is a therapist, who can talk to you about ways to feel more comfortable with your identity in all areas of your life. Try to find a therapist who specializes in LGBTQ issues, as this person will likely have a better understanding of what you are going through. You may also benefit from a support group in your area or a local social group where you can meet others who identify similarly. Building a network of people who understand your experience will make it easier to know when to share and when to stay quiet about your LGBTQ status.

TIMES ARE CHANGING SLOWLY

Despite federal laws for marriage equality, changes for LGBTQ individuals in the workplace are moving slowly. According to *USA Today*, almost half of LGBTQ adults remain closeted at work. This is a percentage that hasn't changed much in the last ten years, as LGBTQ

Marriage equality has made it easier to come out at work.

individuals feel as though there is a double standard in the workplace. While some companies have developed successful diversity-training programs, 53 percent of LGBTQ adults still hear gay or lesbian jokes in the workplace. This makes it very difficult to feel comfortable at work and to come out in any meaningful way.

Marriage equality, which became the law of the land in 2015, has made it easier for some individuals to come out at work since the increased visibility of same-sex couples has fostered more accepting attitudes. In addition, progressive areas of the United States see a higher rate of workers coming out in the workplace than the national average. For individuals who live in a progressive state such as Massachusetts, most feel very comfortable coming out in the workplace. As it was the first state to grant marriage equality to same-sex couples years before marriage equality became federal law, many Massachusetts workers are out to their coworkers and feel comfortable being so.

In 1997, comedian Ellen Degeneres decided that it was time she came out.

Some work environments can be hostile toward those who are different.

WHY LGBTQ INDIVIDUALS DON'T COME OUT AT WORK

Coming out at work is a personal choice. While you may have reasons to come out at work, there are also reasons LGBTQ individuals may decide to remain in the closet at work. Sometimes a work environment

ELLEN'S "PUPPY EPISODE"

In 1997, comedian Ellen Degeneres decided that it was time she came out and identified herself as a lesbian. She did so in a big way, coming out in an episode, "Puppy Episode," where she accidentally states, "I'm gay" into a microphone her character was not aware of. This sparked some backlash for Ellen, but she maintained that it was important for her as a lesbian to come out in support of other gays and lesbians who were also hiding their status.

is hostile toward those who are different. If you hear a joke that targets LGBTQ people, you probably won't feel safe coming out at work. A hostile work environment can stem from a variety of causes, but for those who identify as LGBTQ, it may signal the potential for abuse and discrimination. Still others feel their identity isn't anyone's business, and they choose to keep their lives private.

While increasing numbers of people who identify as straight believe that LGBTQ coworkers should feel free to share their full identity, others insist that a person's sexual orientation or gender identity should be hidden in the workplace. What many straight people don't realize is that one quick "my wife" uttered by a straight man is sharing his identity. Because being straight and cisgender is the traditional and most common identity, it never seems like a shock to talk about a spouse of the opposite sex. But this same statement made by a woman might have very different repercussions in the workplace. A woman referring to "my wife" may be accused of pushing her identity politics on coworkers, even when the statement is casual.

The prejudice surrounding what is normal and acceptable persists.

The prejudice surrounding what is normal and acceptable persists. Almost 60 percent of non-LGBTQ individuals believe that talking about your sexual identity is not appropriate for the workplace. It is an extreme double standard that LGBTQ individuals have to deal with every single day. A straight woman can come into work and share pictures of her family, her children, her husband, and no one will think that it is anything more than simple sharing. If an LGBTQ person were to do the same thing at work, it could open up big problems. Everyone has a sexual identity, but the majority bias is so deeply ingrained in some straight individuals that they can't see how their casual behaviors are constantly identifying their sexuality and gender identities.

COMING OUT NATURALLY AT WORK

It is hard to stay in the closet at work. It can feel as if you have to walk on eggshells around your peers, monitoring everything you say and do and share on social media. This is both stressful and unfair to you. And there may come a time when you slip up and out yourself by accident. If you do, move on with the conversation, and try not to make a big deal out of it. You do not have to explain or defend yourself.

There is never a perfect time to come out at work, though it may be easier if you've gotten to know your colleagues a little first. If you have been at a job for more than a few months, you will begin to develop relationships with other people. As your comfort level with others increases, you will find yourself talking more about who you are. Sometimes you may simply want to share what you did over the weekend. If the environment is casual, and you tend to have lunch breaks with coworkers, chances are that the conversation will become personal. Over time, you will be able to identify people who are going to understand your LGBTQ status.

If you don't feel comfortable coming out at work, that doesn't mean you have to hide who you are. As you learn about your coworkers, it will feel natural for you to begin to share information about your life. You don't have to go into details, and you don't have to share any information you don't feel comfortable sharing.

If you slip up and out yourself by accident, try not to make a big deal out of it.

Coming out at work may be easier if you've gotten to know your coworkers.

As an LGBTQ individual, chances are good that you are going to be outed at work at some point. The best way to try to manage this is to stay calm and not feel as if you ever have to defend who you are. When you *do* want to come out at work, identify a person or two who you believe will feel comfortable with the news. Be casual about your status, and try not to explain yourself in depth. If you are a female who mentions your wife, let the conversation continue to flow. You'll discover who is comfortable with the topic and who doesn't want to discuss it by the reactions you receive.

You are never obligated to come out in the workplace. Your sexual and gender identities are not anyone else's business. That said, it is a good idea to have a plan so that you can come out on your own terms.

Be casual about your status, and try not to over explain.

When you have more control over who you come out to, it can be easier to manage any potential fallout.

Coming out at work can be a challenge, but as you gain confidence in who you are, it will feel like less of a big deal. While you are not obligated to share with your coworkers, it is fair to casually mention your status when others are sharing stories from their personal lives. If you begin to hang out socially with coworkers, it is more likely that you will begin to share your personal life.

When you are an LGBTQ adult in the workplace, you will want to focus on your professional life first. Know what information is appropriate to share with coworkers. If you have become friends with coworkers on social media, pay attention to your privacy settings. One of the fastest ways to be accidentally outed is to share something on social media not intended for work friends. If you are nervous about your sexual identity for any reason, it is best to share very little about that part of your life on social media.

If you have become friends with coworkers on social media, check your privacy settings.

TEXT-DEPENDENT QUESTIONS

1. Whose choice is it to come out at work?

2. How should you react if you are outed at work?

3. What year was it legal for same-sex couples to get married throughout the United States?

RESEARCH PROJECT

Jameka Evans was fired from Georgia Regional Hospital for being a lesbian and filed a lawsuit based on discrimination. The U.S. Supreme Court refused to hear her case in December 2017. Research what protections, if any, on the state and federal level prohibit an employer from firing an employee because they are LGBTQ.

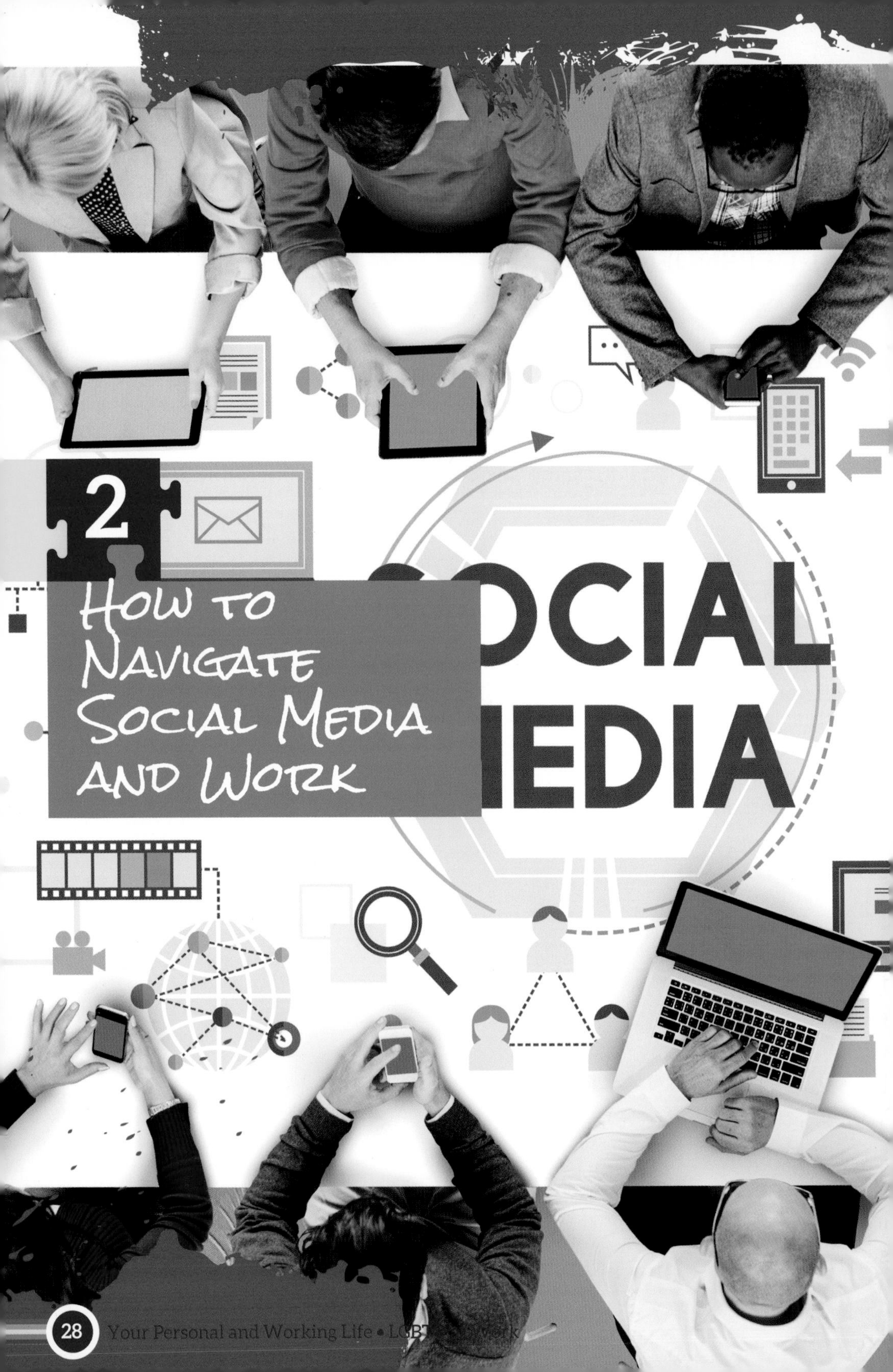

2 How to Navigate Social Media and Work

WORDS TO UNDERSTAND

ACTIVISM: *Activities that you participate in with a primary goal in mind to change a policy, procedure, or law.*

SUBORDINATE: *A person you supervise at work.*

TAGGING: *Identifying person who is shown in an image in order to share the image to their profile on social media.*

How you utilize social media is essentially up to you. The time you spend on social media, the posts you choose to share, and the people who can follow your posts are all aspects of social media that are up to you. When you are an LGBTQ individual and have concerns about your privacy in the workplace, it's time to pay attention to how you use social media and the people you choose to share your life with. The use of social media can make it nearly impossible to have a private life, and it is up to you to set the parameters of social media, or they can take over your life.

CHOOSE YOUR PRIVACY SETTINGS WISELY

There are privacy settings on social media for a reason. You don't have to share a post with the public, even when you want to share it with your friends on social media. Look over the privacy settings. You can make it as simple as sharing only with your friends, or you can create specific lists to share information with. Anything you post on social media can end up in the public eye,

There are privacy settings on social media for a reason.

Working with someone doesn't mean you have to be friends on social media.

but you can take some steps to make it harder to share your content. Know what your privacy settings are, and don't be afraid to block users you don't feel comfortable with.

YOU CAN IGNORE FRIEND REQUESTS

Just because you started working with someone, it doesn't mean you have to become fast friends on social media. If you receive a friend request, you can simply ignore it. If a coworker sends you a friend request the first day of work, and you are concerned about outing yourself as an LGBTQ individual, you don't have to accept the request.

Your public profile name can be something that coworkers won't know.

If you are questioned by the coworker, understand that you don't have to be friends with people on social media just because they ask. You can make a statement such as "Oh, I'm not really on there anymore" if you really feel put on the spot.

CHANGE YOUR PUBLIC PROFILE NAME

When you want your life to remain as private as possible from people at work, your public profile name can be something that coworkers won't know. Some people shorten their last name or use a nickname from growing up to avoid professional relationships on social media. Look at your privacy settings, and make it impossible for others to see who your friends are if you're concerned about privacy issues. That way, it will be hard to narrow down your identity. When you change your name, your current friends will still know who you are, while new people won't know how to find you.

MAKE IT IMPOSSIBLE TO SEARCH FOR YOU

You don't have to allow public searches for your name on social media. As an LGBTQ individual, your privacy may be very important to you. While you have your friends' network set up, you don't have to make it possible for the general public to be able to find you through a search. If you don't want to change your name, you can change your settings so that only your active friends can see you on social media. If a coworker isn't able to search for you on social media, you can avoid the uncomfortable friend request right from the start. If you are looking for a job, making yourself impossible to find on social media is an excellent idea if protecting your privacy is important to you.

LIMIT YOUR PHOTO SHARING

Photos can be a tricky aspect of social media and sharing. A picture of you and a group of friends may seem like no big deal, but if you are trying to hide your LGBTQ status from your coworkers, this can

A photo on social media may contain signs that indicate your status.

quickly become a problem. Within a picture, there may be signs that indicate your status. Maybe someone in the picture has on a gay pride shirt, or there is a same-sex couple in the image holding hands. When you share an image, and you are trying to protect the fact you are LGBTQ, it's important to carefully look over the image before hitting the share button.

PAY ATTENTION TO THE PAGES YOU LIKE OR SHARE

The people you allow to see your profile will know the sites and pages you follow.

When you like a particular page, your followers or friends on social media can see that you do. Go onto a social media site, and take a look for yourself. Pages or groups that your friends like will be shared with you in an effort to get you to like the page, too. If you follow a bunch of LGBTQ-positive sites, the people you allow to see your profile in the first place are going to know about the sites you follow. When you are trying to keep your LGBTQ status under wraps on social media, consider your options when it comes to liking or sharing any content on the site.

LIMIT PARTICIPATION IN PUBLIC GROUPS

Public groups are another way you can end up sharing information you don't want to share with people on social media. If you belong to a public group, everyone who belongs to it can see what you share unless you have specifically blocked an individual. While you may want to be a political activist using social media to improve the rights of the LGBTQ community, this is the fastest way to out yourself to others using social media. If necessary, you can create a separate account for your **activism** to keep this aspect of your life out of the view of your friends and family you want to share simple pictures and stories with.

Using social media for political activism can out you to coworkers on social media.

DON'T ALLOW TAGGING FROM OTHER PEOPLE

Tagging is a simple profile setting, and you don't have to allow others to tag you in a photo without your permission. If you do, then any images anyone takes of you might include your name on them. When you spend time and thought on whether to share a particular image, you don't want to ruin your privacy by having an image of you tagged that you didn't give permission to share. You can set up your social media profile to ask for permission before you allow your name to be attached to any image, no matter who is tagging you. You will have the opportunity to look at the image and decide whether you want it to include your name.

Learn more about social media safety.

You don't have to allow others to tag you in a photo without your permission.

Friending a coworker may be against the policy of your company.

KNOW THE RULES SET BY YOUR WORKPLACE

When it comes to social media, employers have developed policies around the use of social media between peers and **subordinates**. Know the social media policy your employer has established, and make sure that you follow the parameters of the policy. Even if a coworker wants to friend you on social media, this may be against the policy of your company. In general, most companies don't want supervisors to be friends on social media with those they supervise or

There are many reasons to keep your work life and your personal life separate.

with any clients that the company serves. It is always best to use social media at a minimum when you are starting a new job and to be wary of friending anyone you meet within the company.

KEEP YOUR PERSONAL AND WORK LIFE SEPARATE

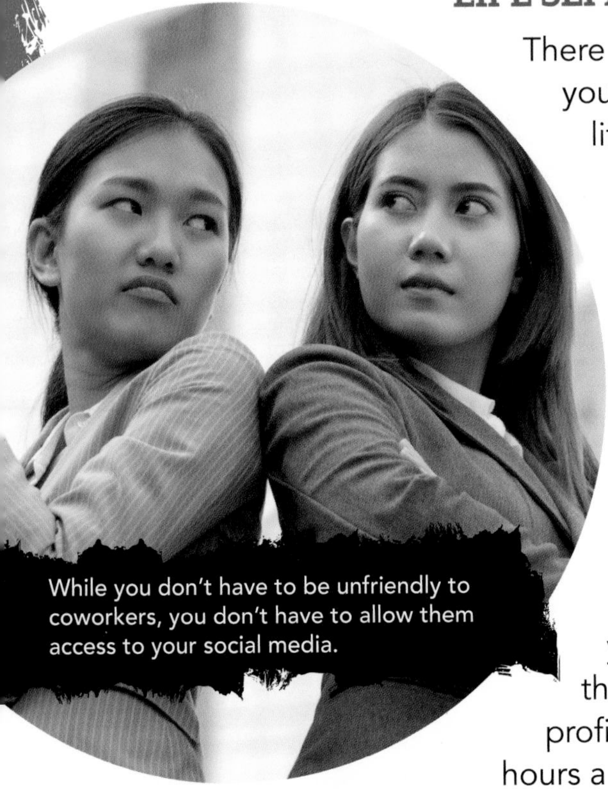

While you don't have to be unfriendly to coworkers, you don't have to allow them access to your social media.

There are many reasons to keep your work life and your personal life separate. When you are an LGBTQ individual, there are even more reasons to allow for this obvious separation to keep you protected. When you first start a job, people will want to know more about who you are. Social media make it easier to learn about you without having to ask you much. People at work have no business friending you on your first day of work, only to then scour through your personal profile to investigate. You spend many hours a week with people from work, and there's no need to share with your coworkers what you choose to share on social media. Most adults recommend keeping your personal and work lives separate to give yourself privacy and a work life that doesn't consume your private life.

PLACE VALUE ON YOUR PRIVACY

Social media etiquette does not require you to share your life story with anyone who has an Internet connection. Your privacy matters. When you consider your own privacy, think about what you would share in the break room at work. If you want to keep a professional distance from your coworkers, it's important to keep coworkers away from your social media profiles. While you don't have to be cold to coworkers, you don't have to allow access to your social media content. When you are an LGBTQ individual, this may prevent you from facing any discrimination in the workplace because of what you put on social media.

No one should be sharing every intimate detail of their lives on social media.

USE COMMON SENSE ON SOCIAL MEDIA

Common sense goes a long way when it comes to using social media. No one should be sharing every intimate detail of their lives. People who need to know your spouse cheated or that you have a strange medical condition you are having checked out are going to be people you tell in person. When you share intimate information on social media, this information can get into the wrong hands. Even simply sharing that you had a rough day at work can become difficult for you if a boss finds out. Social media have changed the way employers screen and monitor employees. Use your common sense, and don't post anything about your employer if you value your job.

Social media have made the workplace more difficult to navigate for LGBTQ people, and most people in general. Social media can be fun and a great way to get to know people better. Problems occur when people who don't have the same level of power within a company become friends on social media. Through social media, a supervisor

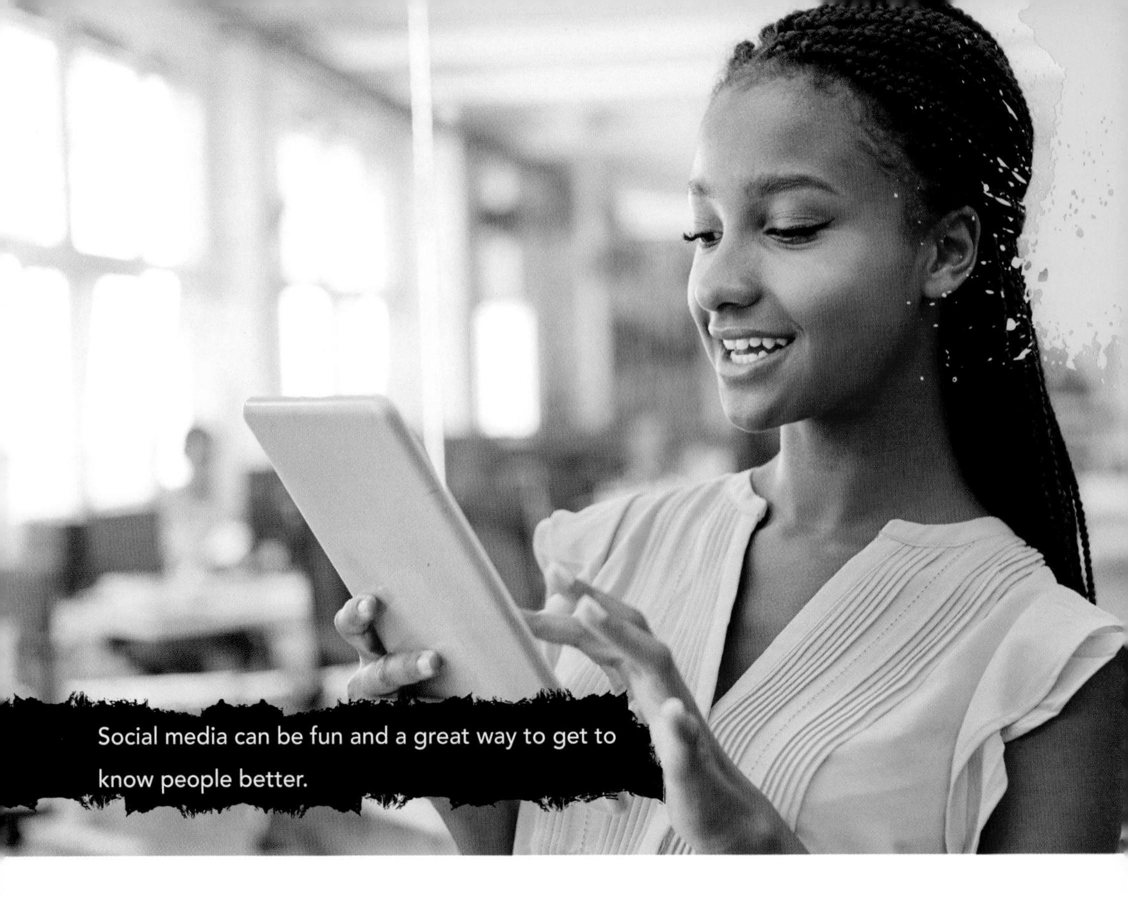
Social media can be fun and a great way to get to know people better.

could learn that a person they supervise wasn't really out sick but out at a concert instead, thus causing a problem at work. Employers often use social media to screen potential employees by simply looking them up and trying to find any information they can. If your employer finds information they don't approve of about you on social media, you can find yourself being let go from your job because of it.

How you use social media will impact your life. If you are trying to keep your LGBTQ status private, it will be easiest to limit your social media use in the first place. When you don't engage in social media, you don't risk outing yourself. If you want to use social media but don't want your status known, you have to be careful at every step of the process. Watch whom you agree to friend, and set all privacy settings that you can. Pay attention to any pictures of you on social media, and remove anything that might be prejudicial. You can use social media safely, but you're going to have to be careful if you're protecting your LGBTQ status.

TEXT-DEPENDENT QUESTIONS

1. When did Facebook first begin, and what social media network did it take over?
2. Should you friend everyone you meet at work who wants to be your friend on social media? Why? Why not?
3. What is a social media use policy?

RESEARCH PROJECT

Talk to one of your parents about their workplace. See whether they are friends with any of their coworkers online. Find out the employer's social media policy, and talk to your parent about whether they agree with the policy and whether they follow it closely.

3

Benefits for Your Partner

WORDS TO UNDERSTAND

DOMESTIC PARTNERSHIP: *Two people in a committed relationship who share money and a home, are over 18 years old, and are not related by blood.*

HEALTH CARE PROXY: *An individual assigned by you in a document whom you state is responsible for making all of your medical decisions if you are not able to do so.*

HEALTH INSURANCE: *Insurance that pays for medical care from doctors, therapists, and other providers without an individual having to pay the full cost of the service.*

Same-sex marriage is now federally recognized in the United States. That means that your spouse is just like any other spouse of a straight person when it comes to receiving employer benefits offered to you as a married individual. If you and your partner are not married, you still may be able to get benefits for your partner if the employer offers partner benefits. Many companies no longer offer same-sex partner benefits, as they recognize that same-sex marriage now exists and would entitle married couples to benefits no matter what sex the individuals in the couple are.

DISCRETION WITH YOUR HUMAN RESOURCES DEPARTMENT

If you are in a same-sex marriage, you might be more comfortable with people at the office knowing of your LGBTQ status. When you are not comfortable with this information being shared at work, it's time to talk with your human resources department about your fears. You may want to sign your spouse up for **health insurance** benefits but still want to keep your LGTBQ status private. The human resources department is not allowed to discuss your private life with anyone. You can let the

The human resources department is not allowed to discuss your private life with anyone.

individual know that you have concerns with others in the workplace finding out about your same-sex partner and that you expect that this information won't be shared.

DOMESTIC PARTNER BENEFITS

The establishment of domestic partner benefits arose over the years because same-sex couples were able to advocate for their own needs and get benefits for the people they were in committed relationships with. Straight couples can also register as **domestic partnerships**, although many simply chose to get married legally instead. There are no federal guidelines as to what a domestic partnership is, and each state has its own set of requirements and benefits that are provided to domestic partners. Vermont was the first state to provide benefits to same-sex domestic partnerships, and some states still use this model

Each state has its own requirements and benefits provided to domestic partners.

Marriage equality became federal law in the United States on June 26, 2015.

to provide benefits to couples who register as domestic partnerships but are not married.

QUALIFYING AS DOMESTIC PARTNERS

With each state having slightly different parameters when it comes to registering as a domestic partnership, it is important to know what the

MARRIAGE EQUALITY: THE LAW OF THE LAND

Marriage equality became federal law in the United States on June 26, 2015. This meant that any state that had a ban on same-sex marriages could no longer discriminate against same-sex couples who wanted to get married. It took six months for the U.S. Supreme Court decision to take full effect throughout the United States, but eventually, same-sex couples were granted marriage licenses throughout all 50 states.

Domestic partners share homes and money, and they might even be raising children together.

rules are in your state in order to get the benefits that you want for your partner. The federal government does not recognize domestic partnerships, so this means that any federal benefits you are entitled to can't go to your partner as well. In general, to qualify as a domestic partnership, you must live as if you were already married. Couples must be in a committed relationship and can be either same-sex or opposite-sex. In the majority of cases, the couple shares a home and money, and they might even live with children they are raising together.

To be considered a domestic partner, both parties must be over 18 years old or older and not be related by blood. Both parties must not be married to other people, and it may be necessary to prove the length of the relationship to seek domestic partner benefits.

In order to make medical decisions for your partner, you have to be legally partnered.

WHY BEING MARRIED OR IN A DOMESTIC PARTNERSHIP MATTERS

When you have a partner you love, there are aspects of your arrangement that you will want to protect. For example, if you are not married or a domestic partner, you don't have rights when it comes to your legally partner if they get sick. This was particularly challenging for same-sex couples who would have problems with their partner's family members refusing them access to their partner while in the hospital. To make medical decisions for your partner, you would have to be married or in a registered domestic partnership.

LGBTQ couples would protect their rights as much as possible by naming each other as **health care proxies**, but this was little protection in an emergency and certainly didn't offer the same benefits that straight, married couples got automatically. By law, same-sex couples weren't allowed to visit each other in the hospital or in jail, or to take time off to bereave the loss of one's partner. With marriage now a viable option for same-sex couples, the rights and responsibilities are comparable to straight couples in marriages.

Carefully consider whether policies are offering the benefits you're looking for.

WHAT DOES IT MEAN TO HAVE DOMESTIC PARTNER BENEFITS?

When you access benefits for your partner at your new job, you will have to talk to your human resources department about what benefits are available. If you are married, your spouse has the same benefits as any other married spouse at the company. Domestic partner benefits may be slightly different, so look over any policies carefully to see whether the benefits are what you are looking for. Your spouse or partner would be able to receive health, dental, and vision insurance. If you have a flexible spending account for medical needs, you can use the money to pay for your spouse to receive care as well. Flexible spending accounts allow you to save a portion of your earnings in a pre-taxed account, and you can use the money for any medical needs that you have. If you have life insurance through work, you still will want to name your spouse or partner as the beneficiary if that's whom you want benefits to go to should you pass away.

WHEN YOU ARE NERVOUS ABOUT YOUR LGBTQ STATUS

While the world has come a long way in accepting those who are not straight, this does not mean that everyone feels safe coming out in the workplace. If you are nervous about sharing your LGBTQ status, talk with your supervisor. Most human resources departments have the skills necessary to make you feel comfortable about signing your

As an LGBTQ individual, you have the same rights as everyone else.

If you are married, you have the right to be at the bedside of your sick spouse.

partner up for the benefits you both deserve. As an LGBTQ individual, you have the same rights as everyone else working in the company. You can't be fired for your sexual orientation, in some states. You can't have benefits withheld from your same-sex spouse, because these marriages are now federally recognized.

SICK LEAVE TO TAKE CARE OF YOUR SAME-SEX PARTNER

If you are married, you have the right to be at the bedside of your spouse if they are sick or in the hospital. Family medical leave is established so that workers can take time off from work to care for a sick family member, without fear of losing their job. If you need to leave work to take care of your same-sex domestic partner, this might be more difficult for you. If you and your partner are not in a registered domestic partnership, and you are not married, your employer does not have to allow you to take family medical leave of

Be honest with your employer if an emergency arises, and do what you need for your partner.

absence to care for your sick partner. If you are married, or your state allows you to register as a domestic partnership, you are allowed to take the time off.

Many employers are not going to punish you for needing to take time off to care for a sick partner, but you may have to be upfront about your LGBTQ status if a situation occurs. If human resources doesn't know about your live-in partner, it may take some explaining for you to get the time off that you need. Be honest with your employer if an emergency arises, and do what you need to in order to be there for your partner.

Some employers are not allowed to discriminate against you based on your choice of partner or your LGBTQ status. You may find an employer who doesn't discriminate based on your LGBTQ status, even if your state doesn't have laws to protect you. Refusing you time off to be with a distressed partner is a form of discrimination that you may need to fight further down the road. When you are upfront with your employer, they might be understanding about your relationship status.

Many LGBTQ couples before you fought for marriage equality and rights.

GETTING THE BENEFITS YOU DESERVE

Now that it is legal for two consenting adults to get married and receive benefits regardless of sexual orientation, it's time to stand up for your rights. If you are married but worried about what your employer will think about your same-sex partner, it will help to have confidence in your relationship. You may discover that the environment where you work is supportive to LGBTQ individuals and that you had no reason to be concerned. Your spouse is entitled to receive benefits because they are married to you, and that can mean significant savings if you both don't need to have individual health insurance plans. Understand that many same-sex couples have gone before you to fight for this very right, and you should receive any benefits you and your spouse are entitled to without fear of everyone at the company finding out about your marital status.

You and your partner deserve to live a life free of discrimination.

Many couples have one partner whose job offers better health insurance, flexible spending accounts, and other benefits. For people in straight marriages, there is no question that one person would sign up for benefits under the person with the good job offering better insurance. For same-sex couples, the ability to do so is new and can feel overwhelming.

While you may be trying to keep your LGBTQ status to yourself, this doesn't mean you have to miss out on benefits that are important for you as a couple. Health insurance and medical costs can be expensive, and same-sex couples are now better able to manage financially because of benefits of federally recognized marriages and

A family health insurance plan will cover you, your spouse, and your children.

benefits offered to spouses. Your company is under an obligation to keep your personal information within the human resources department. If you discover that you have been outed because you signed up your same-sex partner for benefits, you may have legal options to consider.

You shouldn't be afraid about being outed at work, but that can be hard for you to overcome. You and your partner deserve to live a life free of discrimination, but anyone living in the real world knows that that isn't always the case. Your partner is entitled to receive benefits based on your employment, if they are offered, and your company may not share your information with anyone.

As you consider what benefits to sign up for, look at your overall financial picture. It may be easier for your partner to obtain benefits through their own job. In many opposite-sex couples, each individual carries their own individual insurance plan because it is a cheaper option for the couple. Once children are in the mix, a family plan is generally the most affordable option for any family.

If you and your spouse have children together, you will want to look at family plans to see how much they will cost you each month. A family plan will cover you, your spouse, and your children, and it will be the most affordable way for you to have health insurance benefits for your entire family. Even if you are a bit nervous about signing up for benefits, you are likely to discover that human resources is very comfortable dealing with your exact situation.

TEXT-DEPENDENT QUESTIONS

1. Have domestic partnership benefits been replaced by benefits for married couples?

2. Why were domestic partnerships established?

3. What was the first state to allow benefits for same-sex partners?

RESEARCH PROJECT

Learn more about domestic partner benefits in your state. Does your state offer domestic partnerships? Did your state ever offer domestic partner benefits? What would you need to do to register as a domestic partnership in your state?

4
Discrimination in the Workplace

WORDS TO UNDERSTAND

CISGENDERED: *An individual whose gender identity matches their birth gender.*

GENDER IDENTITY: *The gender, or non-gender, distinction that an individual chooses to be called.*

PRIVATE SECTOR: *Private companies, as distinguished from nonprofit entities or public establishments such as schools, towns, or municipalities.*

One of the major reasons LGBTQ individuals want to keep their status private is the potential of facing discrimination in the workplace. While most people have one reason or another for which they could be discriminated against at work, LGBTQ individuals see a higher rate of overall discrimination in the workplace than anyone else. It is estimated that 10 percent of LGBTQ employees have left a job at one point because the environment they were working in was not welcoming. While times have changed, and workplaces have become more welcoming for LGBTQ individuals, there is still a lot of work to be done.

LGBTQ DISCRIMINATION AT WORK

Employees who identify as LGBTQ have a higher rate of reported discrimination cases than individuals of other groups often discriminated against. In the last five years alone, 1 in 4 LGBTQ employees has reported incidents of discrimination at work. For individuals who are transgender, the rate is even higher. Transgender individuals are the group most likely to try to avoid mistreatment at work by not sharing their transgender identity. At least 10 percent of LGBTQ workers have left a job at some point because the company was not welcoming to LGBTQ people.

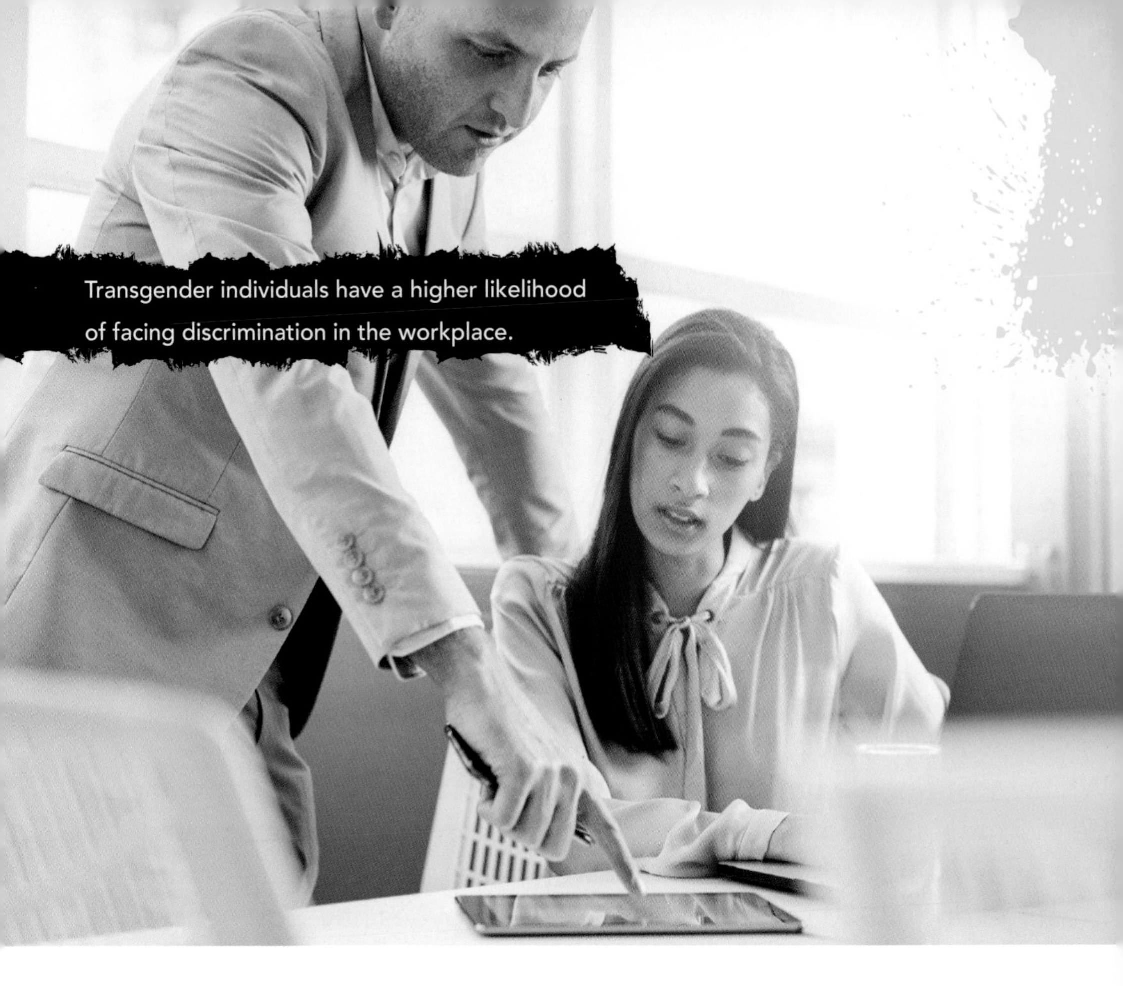

Transgender individuals have a higher likelihood of facing discrimination in the workplace.

WHEN A COWORKER DISCOVERS YOUR LGBTQ STATUS

If a coworker finds out your LGBTQ status, it will benefit you overall to try and remain calm. Most people are tolerant, and finding out that you are a lesbian, gay, or transgender might not matter at all to your coworker. If you feel comfortable enough with the person, let them know that your status is not widely shared at the office. The person may have trouble accepting your status, and that might mean you will have to talk with your human resources department. While you may be nervous, try to remain casual about the discovery. You have done nothing wrong by being LGBTQ, and it is not up to you to defend your status.

Discrimination at work could be due to a variety of factors.

WHAT DOES IT MEAN TO BE DISCRIMINATED AGAINST?

Discrimination can occur at any time, and the reason for the discrimination could be factors as varied as **gender identity**, sexual orientation, race, ethnicity, religious preference, age, and more. For simplicity, consider that an older person comes in looking for a job at your company. The individual is highly qualified and would be perfect for the position. A younger person is hired for the job, because the person hiring doesn't want to supervise someone who is older than they are. If the person was not hired because of their age, that is considered age discrimination.

Is an LGBTQ-insensitive joke discrimination or just offensive?

The biggest problem with discrimination is that it can be very hard to prove. Intent matters when it comes to discrimination, and there are a lot of ways that harmless communication can be misinterpreted. In an LGBTQ example, if a supervisor calls you a derogatory name based on your sexual identity and writes you up for something you didn't do, that is discriminatory. On the other hand, what happens if a coworker tells a LGBTQ-insensitive joke?

There are many times that LGBTQ individuals blow off a joke aimed at their identity, especially if the people they are working with are not aware of their status. It is not always safe to stick up for those who are

Employee resource groups help to foster inclusivity in the workplace.

If a joke makes you feel uncomfortable, and you speak up, you may be accused of being too sensitive.

marginalized, and a seemingly harmless joke can be very offensive. It is hard to determine what is discrimination rather than merely in poor taste. While you shouldn't have to be in a workplace where you don't feel safe, it can be hard to determine what makes you feel unsafe in the first place.

HAVE PEOPLE BECOME TOO SENSITIVE?

People who claim they are only joking when they make a racist or homophobic joke may state that you are too sensitive if you call them out about the joke. Even when your feelings are hurt, or a joke makes you feel uncomfortable, you may be accused of being too sensitive. That is not a fair statement, but it is something you are likely to encounter if you bring up how inappropriate a homophobic joke is. If you are in a comfortable work environment, it won't be as hard for you to talk about a joke that offends you. When the environment is not a comfortable place for you, it may be very difficult for you to bring up your concerns when a joke is told that makes fun of who you are. In general, people are more open to the fact that racist or homophobic jokes are wrong, and they are more likely to say something when such a joke is told.

PROTECTIONS FOR LGBTQ INDIVIDUALS AT WORK

While things have improved for LGBTQ individuals, they are far from equal when it comes to being LGBTQ in the workplace. There are no federal laws that protect LGBTQ individuals at work based on sexual orientation or gender identity. Federal laws that would prohibit employers throughout the United States from firing, or not hiring, an individual based on their sexual orientation don't exist. Some states have established laws to protect LGBTQ individuals at work, but so far only 22 states and the District of Columbia have established laws that prohibit discrimination at work based on a person's gender identity or sexuality.

The laws to protect LGBTQ individuals are weak throughout most of the United States. In 28 states, you can be fired for coming out as

The laws to protect LGBTQ individuals are weak throughout most of the United States.

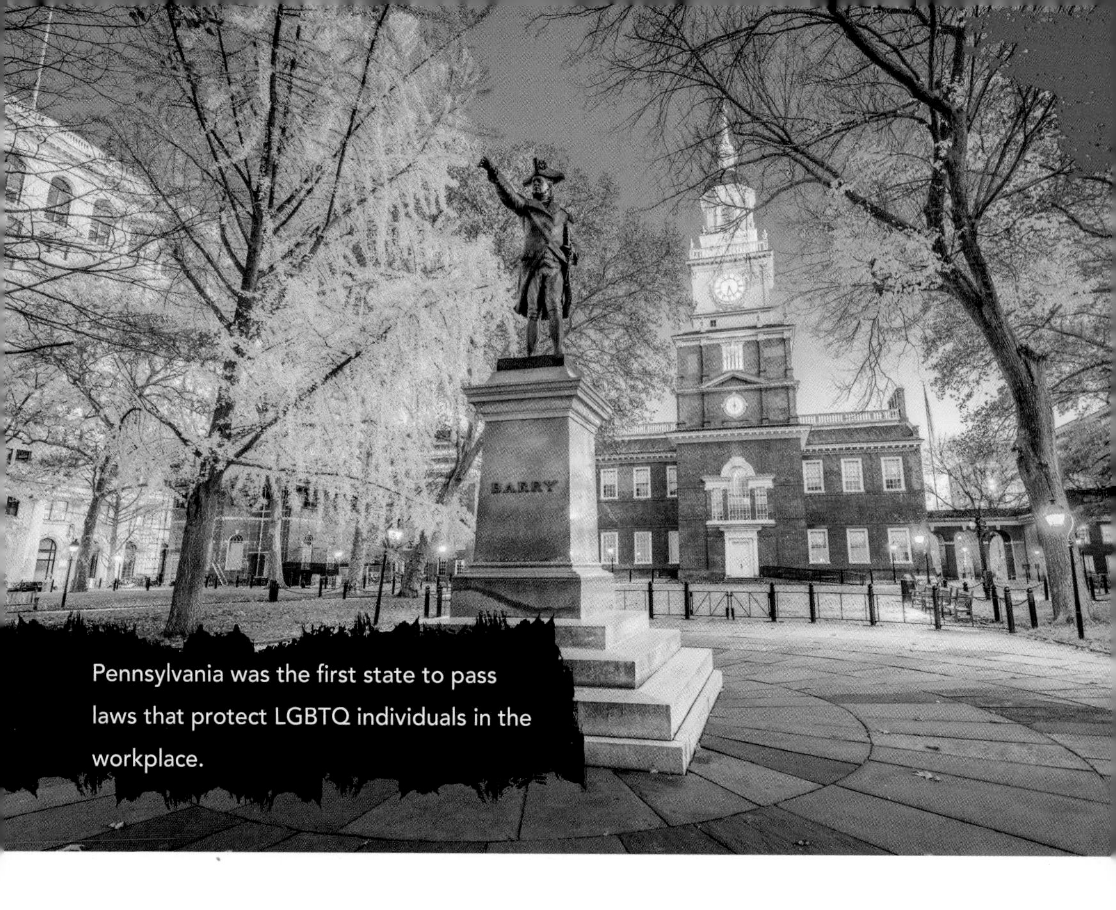

Pennsylvania was the first state to pass laws that protect LGBTQ individuals in the workplace.

lesbian, gay, or bisexual, a major reason LGBTQ people are afraid to have their status discovered. Although many Americans support laws that protect LGBTQ people from discrimination at work, the laws are not there to protect people from discrimination simply because of their gender identity.

Legal Protections in the Workplace

Pennsylvania was the first state to pass laws that protect LGBTQ individuals in the workplace. Back in 1975, Pennsylvania banned public-sector discrimination of LGBTQ individuals, while the state passed similar protective legislation by 1982 for the **private sector** as well. Despite these early advancements for the rights of the LGBTQ community, in 2018 there are still no federal protections for this class of people.

Take a careful look at your company's discrimination policy.

FIND OUT WHAT YOUR OFFICE DISCRIMINATION POLICY IS

Take a careful look at your company's discrimination policy to determine what, if any, your protections are as an LGBTQ person. If you live in a state that protects LGBTQ individuals, this should be apparent in your company's discrimination policy. If there is no language in your company's policy that addresses sexual orientation or gender identity, you may have to do some further investigation. As of 2019, the places where LGBTQ workers are protected are the District of Columbia, Maine, Massachusetts, California, Vermont, Oregon, Rhode Island, Connecticut, New Hampshire, New York, New Jersey, Maryland, Illinois, Hawaii, Washington, Minnesota, Iowa, Nevada, Utah, New Mexico, and Colorado. Sadly, the rest of the United States does not offer such protection.

It doesn't matter who you are. You deserve to feel safe at work.

CONSIDER YOUR OWN SITUATION

It doesn't matter whether you are **cisgendered**, genderqueer, lesbian, gay, or gender neutral—you deserve to feel safe in the place where you work. Unfortunately, the laws to protect LGBTQ individuals are lacking in many areas. If you don't feel safe at work, or if you feel that you are being discriminated against because of your LGBTQ status, it's time to talk with someone who can help you. If you are let go from a job because your supervisor discovered your LGBTQ status, first you have to know whether you are protected against firing in your state for being LGBTQ. If you are protected, you have the right to file a discrimination lawsuit against your employer.

If you experience discrimination at work, document the behaviors that are offensive to you.

For many LGBTQ individuals, the cost of a legal battle is generally prohibitive to filing a discrimination suit. In many states, even if you are protected as an LGBTQ individual, your employer may be able to fire you for any reason at all, even for no reason. In states where you are an employee at will, your employer does not have to give a reason as to why you were fired. Even if you feel that you faced discrimination, you will have to come up with the proof that being an LGBTQ individual was the reason you were fired in the first place.

PROVING DISCRIMINATION AT WORK OCCURRED

If you are feeling harassed at work, or you believe that the environment is becoming hostile to LGBTQ individuals, take your concerns to the human resources department. Their job is to listen to concerns that any employee has and to document the concerns. In addition, they should investigate your concerns. In states that are more progressive, the human resources department is likely to take your concerns more seriously. No matter where you work, if you want to keep your job, and you fear discrimination, document the behaviors that are offensive to you. If a pattern of behavior emerges, it will be easier for you to prove that the environment was hostile to LGBTQ individuals.

YOUR RIGHTS WHEN YOU ARE DISCRIMINATED AGAINST

The Human Rights Campaign and Lambda Legal can provide tools to fight a discrimination case.

When you face discrimination at work, you may have some recourse if you live in a state that protects LGBTQ individuals. The Human Rights Campaign may be able to provide you with assistance in finding legal support in your state. When your human resources department doesn't support you, it's time to reach out for help. Lambda Legal is another national resource that can provide you with the right tools to fight a discrimination case. You are supposed to be able to go to work in an environment where you feel safe and supported, no matter who you are. If you are fired from your job because of discrimination, you may have very few rights to seek damages because of being fired. You probably will be able to collect unemployment benefits, but proving discrimination and fighting against your employer could take years. If you are trying to protect your LGBTQ status, then filing a lawsuit is probably not in your best interest.

Discrimination is likely to occur at some point in your professional life.

Discrimination is likely to occur at some point in your professional life. Whether you are turned down for a promotion because of your LGBTQ status or you hear homophobic jokes in the break room, you probably will feel uncomfortable at some point when you are at work. It will benefit you to pay attention to potential discrimination without outing yourself at the same time. While you might not always be able to do anything about being discriminated against, it is important to pay attention to what goes on where you work.

If you live in a state that doesn't protect LGBTQ individuals in the workplace, you'll have to do some investigation before deciding to work at a particular company. While your state might not protect you against discrimination, the company you work for might. You might learn that a company in your area is very supportive of LGBTQ rights and that it would be an excellent place for you to work if you find a job that matches your qualifications.

As time moves on, the LGBTQ community continues to fight for the rights that every straight, cisgendered individual already receives. Eventually, LGBTQ individuals will feel more comfortable and protected while at work in all 50 states. Until that time, pay attention to the cues you receive in your workplace. If you have any concerns, try to address them with your human resources department.

The LGBTQ community continues to fight for the rights that every straight individual receives.

When you find yourself working in a place that is not supportive of LGBTQ rights, but you can't really identify a way in which you are facing discrimination, it is probably best to find a different job where you will feel comfortable. While rights are becoming more normal for LGBTQ individuals, you don't have to remain at a job where you don't feel accepted or protected by your employer.

TEXT-DEPENDENT QUESTIONS

1. What was the first state to establish protection for LGBTQ workers?
2. Do any federal laws protect LGBTQ workers?
3. What is a discrimination policy?

RESEARCH PROJECT

Take a look at the laws protecting LGBTQ individuals in your state. Have any laws been passed to protect workers who identify as LGBTQ? If not, have any bills been proposed in an effort to establish these laws?

5

Loving Where You Work

WORDS TO UNDERSTAND

ANTI-GAY LEGISLATION: *Potential laws that promote hate toward the LGBTQ community.*

COLLABORATION: *Working together on a project.*

FREELANCER: *A person who works on their own, taking on projects instead of working for a company.*

IDENTIFYING YOUR STRENGTHS

When you want to love where you work, you have to discover what your strengths are. If you take a job just to pay the bills, you will burn out quickly in the position. If you are new to the working world, you'll want to be able to identify what your strengths are to a potential employer. Whether you are highly organized or creative, it's time to learn what your strengths are and what you can bring to any position you seek. When you know who you are and what you have to offer, it becomes easier to find a job that is a good match for you.

FINDING SUITABLE EMPLOYMENT

As an LGBTQ individual, you will want to find a company to work for that has a positive reputation for being LGBTQ-friendly. If you want to try **freelance** work, you'll still want to look for ways you won't be discriminated against, or find work where your sexual orientation doesn't matter. You don't have to out yourself to clients you work with. There are many freelance careers in which you will have minimal contact with clients at all. Find employment that is fulfilling to you, and it will become easier to decide what type of company you want to work for. While it may take you time to find work that you enjoy,

You will want to find a company to work for that is LGBTQ-friendly.

and a company that is friendly to LGBTQ individuals, it will be worth the effort.

TRYING OUT NEW OPPORTUNITIES

To find what you truly love for work, you will want to try out new opportunities that come your way. You won't be able to find out whether you love something if you don't give the job a try. You never know what will happen when you invest some time in looking for work that you will love. Don't be afraid of being true to yourself and what your vision is for your future. You have the ability to reach for your dreams, even if you fear that your LGBTQ status will hold you back. When you accept yourself as an LGBTQ individual, it will become easier for others to do the same. As you start working, try to be true to who you are as a person.

Reach for your dreams even if you fear your LGBTQ status will hold you back.

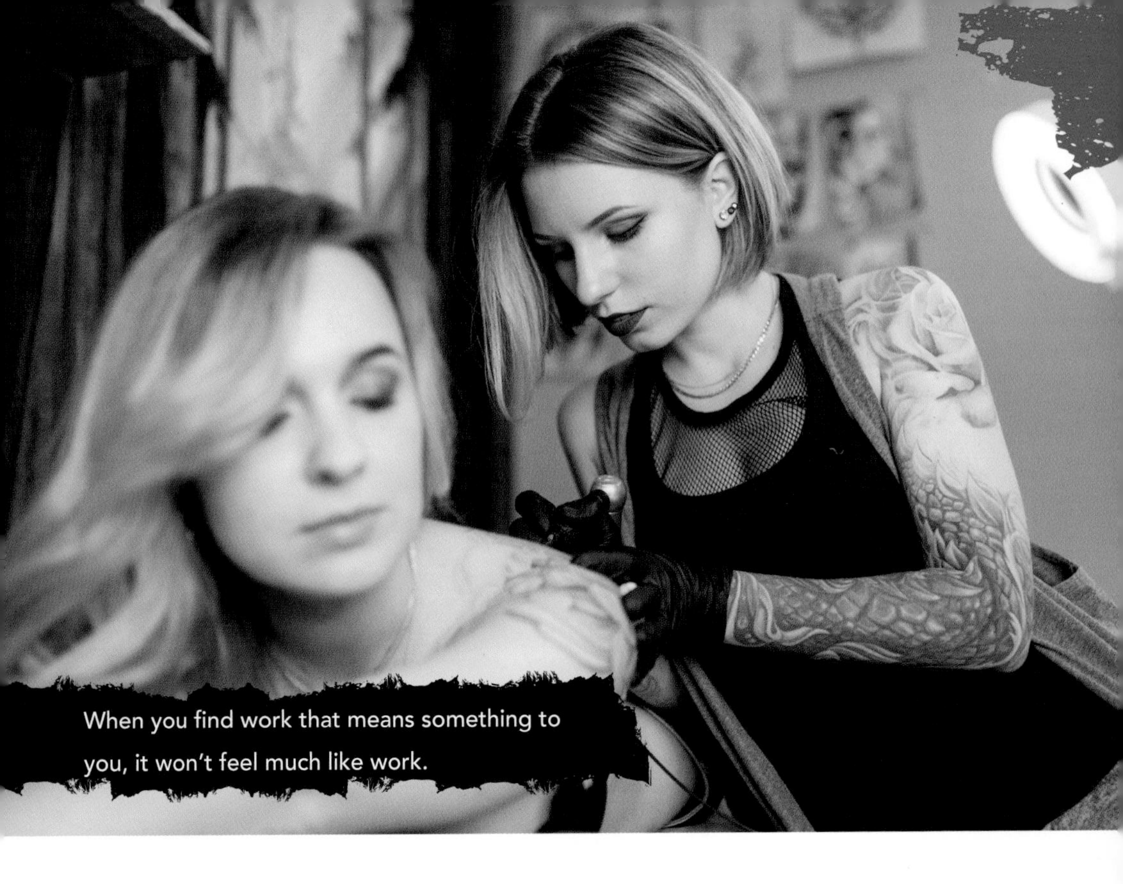
When you find work that means something to you, it won't feel much like work.

TEST OUT THE COMPANY CULTURE

If you are not sure about working at a company, you can always try to find a job within the company on a temporary basis. You won't have to commit to the company, but you'll be able to learn about the culture and how it is to work there. When you are hired on a temporary basis, it gives both you and the employer an opportunity to try one another out. If you don't feel comfortable where you are working, you can seek to move on to another opportunity.

FIND WORK THAT MEANS SOMETHING TO YOU

While you might be trying to find work that gives you a big bank account, over the years, this is not going to give you the fulfillment you are seeking. When you find work that means something to you, it won't feel much like work. If you are an LGBTQ individual, you probably don't want to work for a company that is outwardly homophobic or donates large sums of money to promote **anti-gay legislation**. If you

Take the time to get to know your coworkers and create a healthy work environment.

find a company that supports LGBTQ rights, it will be worth it to see whether you can find a job within that company. When you work for a place that has an agenda in line with what you believe in, it becomes easier to go to work each day.

Watch this video for job tips from LGBTQ leaders.

CREATE AN LGBTQ-FRIENDLY WORK ENVIRONMENT

When you are already in a position, there's no reason you can't use methods to promote an LGBTQ-friendly work environment. Even if you don't want to share your status as an LGBTQ individual, you can start

To learn more about what you love for work, try volunteering in your community.

by talking positively about those who might be different. Be mindful about whom you are talking to at work, and look for opportunities to show that you have an open mind when it comes to people who are not the same as you. Take the time to get to know your coworkers on some level, and create an environment that is conducive to a healthy work environment.

DISCOVER WHAT MAKES YOU UNIQUE

As you look for work opportunities as an LGBTQ individual, it helps to know what makes you stand out as a job candidate. In a tight job market, it becomes even harder to find work that is right for you. When you take a good look at yourself and identify your strengths, it will be easier to identify the job opportunities that are good matches. If you are new to working, it may take you some time to figure out what your strengths are. To learn more about who you are and what you love for work, try volunteering at a variety of organizations in your community.

Even having a positive attitude can help improve the overall morale at work.

That will help you see what types of environments you enjoy and will give you an idea as to the types of people you might want to work with.

BUILD A POSITIVE COMPANY CULTURE

As you work to promote inclusivity, you will help promote a positive company culture. You don't have to be open about your own status as an LGBTQ individual if you aren't comfortable doing so, but you can make it easier on others to come out. The more people who feel comfortable coming out at work, the more positive a work environment it will be. Share your professional goals, and look for ways to build more **collaboration** opportunities between coworkers. Even having a positive attitude can help improve the overall morale where you work. You will find that the more you are yourself, the easier it will be to be out at work eventually. You don't have to share your personal information if you don't want to, but it can come out naturally when you are a positive, upbeat addition to the office.

LOOK FOR WAYS TO IMPROVE DIVERSITY AWARENESS

Diversity awareness is important at work. If you work in a company culture that doesn't promote diversity awareness, it may be time to talk to your human resources department. While you don't have to be responsible for teaching diversity, you have the right to ask about potential training that could improve the company culture. There are all types of people in the world, and when your company only hires or talks about one culture, it can be a boring, sterile place. Instead of getting upset at coworkers who aren't very aware of diversity, try using a more useful approach. While the changes in the office environment may be slow, you can have an impact on the overall culture at work.

When you are comfortable being yourself, it becomes easier for others to accept you for who you are.

BE YOURSELF AT WORK

The best way to find a job you love is to always be yourself. If you are new to the LGBTQ community, that can feel overwhelming. When you are comfortable being yourself, it becomes easier for others to accept who you are. Even in some of the most conservative environments, you should feel confident being the person you are. When you are true to yourself, you will have an easier time finding a job that is a perfect match for you. Let people know who you are, without having to share every

If you can't find what you're looking for within a company, consider a freelance career.

detail of your life, and you will be able to find a job you will love where you will feel comfortable.

KNOW THE CHAIN OF COMMAND

The chain of command at any workplace means the people you talk to if you identify a problem or experience an issue with another worker. In general, the first person you would speak to about an issue would be your immediate supervisor. If the problem is with your supervisor, you would talk to their supervisor. If you aren't sure what the chain of command is within a company, talk to someone from the human resources department. You can ask what the chain of command is for your specific job title, and then follow it if a problem arises. When you follow the right protocol to file a complaint, you will be taken more seriously.

As an employee at any company, you can find job satisfaction if you are in the right environment. If you find yourself bored or don't see any room for advancement, you may need to move on from the company you are working for. Job satisfaction is personal, and knowing what you want out of a job can make a big difference. If you can't find what you are looking for within a company, consider a freelance career where you can develop your own business from the ground up.

THE RISING FREELANCE ECONOMY

While job satisfaction is not always a primary reason to stay at a job, an increasing number of people are demanding more from their work environment. With workers wanting more control of their lives, many are opting to work a in freelance career rather than a traditional office position. It is estimated that roughly 50 percent of the workforce in the United States will be composed of freelance workers by 2020. Freelance work has changed the employment landscape, providing talented individuals with opportunities they would not have if they were stuck in a 9-to-5 position.

Roughly 50 percent of the workforce in the United States will be freelance by 2020.

As you learn more about the company that you work for, don't be afraid to be yourself.

Times have changed for the LGBTQ community in the workplace. People are more open, and diversity is more discussed overall. Even if your home state doesn't have laws that protect LGBTQ individuals, the company you work for might have strong policies in place to protect your rights. As you learn more about the company you are working for, don't be afraid to be yourself. While you don't have to out yourself as an LGBTQ person, you don't have to hide it either. Just allow yourself to act naturally around others and be your best self when you are at work.

When you find an environment you feel safe in, you will begin to understand the importance of professional boundaries. While you might share a little about your personal life, you can see a difference between sharing some information and bringing all of your problems in to work. Being a professional means knowing when it's time to stop sharing and to move on with the work you have in front of you.

It takes time to develop professional boundaries, and you are likely to make mistakes. Boundaries take skill, and if you are new to the work

It takes time to develop professional boundaries, and you are likely to make mistakes along the way.

Rights for LGBTQ people have been slowly and steadily coming.

environment, then it is going to take some practice with learning how to have solid boundaries with your coworkers. Pay attention to those around you. If you have questions, talk to your immediate supervisor. When you are new, your supervisor will expect that you have plenty of questions about the work environment. You will learn your way, and eventually, you will feel more comfortable being an LGBTQ individual, no matter where you work.

With same-sex marriage legal nationwide, it is possible that other protections for LGBTQ individuals will eventually become so as well. Rights for LGBTQ people have been slowly and steadily coming, and equality in the workplace is another hurdle that must be overcome for everyone working and living in the United States.

TEXT-DEPENDENT QUESTIONS

1. What does it mean to be diversity aware?

2. What is the difference between an employee and a freelancer?

3. When you know your strengths, is it easier to find a job?

RESEARCH PROJECT

Locate a company you are interested in working for. Ask whether they have a policy regarding how the LGBTQ community is treated. If they don't have one, does it make you wonder why they don't? If they do, is it specific enough to address the issues that are often present for an LGBTQ person at work?

Series Glossary of Key Terms

Agender (or neutrois, gender neutral, or genderless): Referring to someone who has little or no personal connection with gender.

Ally: Someone who supports equal civil rights, gender equality, and LGBTQ social movements; advocates on behalf of others; and challenges fear and discrimination in all its forms.

Asexual: An adjective used to describe people who do not experience sexual attraction. A person can also be aromantic, meaning they do not experience romantic attraction.

Asexual, or ace: Referring to someone who experiences little or no sexual attraction, or who experiences attraction but doesn't feel the need to act it out sexually. Many people who are asexual still identify with a specific sexual orientation.

Bigender: Referring to someone who identifies with both male and female genders, or even a third gender.

Binary: The belief that such things as gender identity have only two distinct, opposite, and disconnected forms. For example, the belief that only male and female genders exist. As a rejection of this belief, many people embrace a non-binary gender identity. (See **Gender nonconforming.**)

Biphobia: Fear of bisexuals, often based on stereotypes, including inaccurate associations with infidelity, promiscuity, and transmission of sexually transmitted infections.

Bisexual, or bi: Someone who is attracted to those of their same gender as well as to those of a different gender (for example, a woman who is attracted to both women and men). Some people use the word bisexual as an umbrella term to describe individuals that are attracted to more than one gender. In this way, the term is closely related to pansexual, or omnisexual, meaning someone who is attracted to people of any gender identity.

Butch, or masc: Someone whose gender expression is masculine. *Butch* is sometimes used as a derogatory term for lesbians, but it can also be claimed as an affirmative identity label.

Cisgender, or cis: A person whose gender identity matches the gender they were assigned at birth.

Coming out: The process through which a person accepts their sexual orientation and/or gender identity as part of their overall identity. For many, this involves sharing that identity with others, which makes it more of a lifetime process rather than just a one-time experience.

Cross-dresser: While anyone may wear clothes associated with a different sex, the term is typically used to refer to men who occasionally wear clothes, makeup, and accessories that are culturally associated with women. Those men typically identify as heterosexual. This activity is a form of gender expression and not done for entertainment purposes. Cross-dressers do not wish to permanently change their sex or live full-time as women.

Drag: The act of presenting as a different gender, usually for the purpose of entertainment (i.e., drag kings and queens). Many people who do drag do not wish to present as a different gender all of the time.

Gay: Someone who is attracted to those of their same gender. This is often used as an umbrella term but is used more specifically to describe men who are attracted to men.

Gender affirmation surgery: Medical procedures that some individuals elect to undergo to change their physical appearance to resemble more closely the way they view their gender identity.

Gender expression: The external manifestations of gender, expressed through such things as names, pronouns, clothing, haircuts, behavior, voice, and body characteristics.

Gender identity: One's internal, deeply held sense of gender. Some people identify completely with the gender they were assigned at birth (usually male or female), while others may identify with only a part of that gender or not at all. Some people identify with another gender entirely. Unlike gender expression, gender identity is not visible to others.

Gender nonconforming: Referring to someone whose gender identity and/or gender expression does not conform to the cultural or social expectations of gender, particularly in relation to male or female. This can be an umbrella term for many identities, including, but not limited to:

> **Genderfluid:** Someone whose gender identity and/or expression varies over time.
>
> **Genderqueer (or third gender):** Someone whose gender identity and/or expression falls between or outside of male and female.

Heterosexual: An adjective used to describe people whose enduring physical, romantic, and/ or emotional attraction is to people of the opposite sex. Also **straight**.

Homophobia: Fear of people who are attracted to the same sex. *Intolerance*, *bias*, or *prejudice* are usually more accurate descriptions of antipathy toward LGBTQ people.

Intergender: Referring to someone whose identity is between genders and/or a combination of gender identities and expressions.

Intersectionality: The idea that multiple identities intersect to create a whole that is different from its distinct parts. To understand someone, it is important to acknowledge that each of their identities is important and inextricably linked with all of the others. These can include identities related to gender, race, socioeconomic status, ethnicity, nationality, sexual orientation, religion, age, mental and/or physical ability, and more.

Intersex: Referring to someone who, due to a variety of factors, has reproductive or sexual anatomy that does not seem to fit the typical definitions for the female or male sex. Some people who are intersex may identify with the gender assigned to them at birth, while many others do not.

Lesbian: A woman who is attracted to other women. Some lesbians prefer to identify as gay women.

LGBTQ: Acronym for lesbian, gay, bisexual, transgender, and queer or questioning.

Non-binary and/or genderqueer: Terms used by some people who experience their gender identity and/or gender expression as falling outside the categories of man and woman. They may define their gender as falling somewhere in between man and woman, or they may define it as wholly different from these terms.

Out: Referring to a person who self-identifies as LGBTQ in their personal, public, and/or professional lives.

Pangender: Referring to a person whose identity comprises all or many gender identities and expressions.

Pride: The celebration of LGBTQ identities and the global LGBTQ community's resistance against discrimination and violence. Pride events are celebrated in many countries around the world, usually during the month of June to commemorate the Stonewall Riots that began in New York City in June 1969, a pivotal moment in the modern LGBTQ movement.

Queer: An adjective used by some people, particularly younger people, whose sexual orientation is not exclusively heterosexual (e.g., queer person, queer woman). Typically, for those who identify as queer, the terms *lesbian*, *gay*, and *bisexual* are perceived to be too limiting and/or fraught with cultural connotations that they feel don't apply to them. Some people may use *queer*, or more commonly *genderqueer*, to describe their gender identity and/or gender expression (see **non-binary** and/or **genderqueer**). Once considered a pejorative term, *queer* has been reclaimed by some LGBT people to describe themselves; however, it is not a universally accepted term, even within the LGBT community. When Q is seen at the end of LGBT, it may mean *queer* or *questioning*.

Questioning: A time in many people's lives when they question or experiment with their gender expression, gender identity, and/or sexual orientation. This experience is unique to everyone; for some, it can last a lifetime or be repeated many times over the course of a lifetime.

Sex: At birth, infants are commonly assigned a sex. This is usually based on the appearance of their external anatomy and is often confused with gender. However, a person's sex is actually a combination of bodily characteristics including chromosomes, hormones, internal and external reproductive organs, and secondary sex characteristics. As a result, there are many more sexes than just the binary male and female, just as there are many more genders than just male and female.

Sex reassignment surgery: See **Gender affirmation surgery**.

Sexual orientation: A person's enduring physical, romantic, and/or emotional attraction to another person. Gender identity and sexual orientation are not the same. Transgender people may be straight, lesbian, gay, bisexual, or queer. For example, a person who transitions from male to female and is attracted solely to men would typically identify as a straight woman.

Straight, or heterosexual: A word to describe women who are attracted to men and men who are attracted to women. This is not exclusive to those who are cisgender. For example, transgender men may identify as straight because they are attracted to women.

They/Them/Their: One of many sets of gender-neutral singular pronouns in English that can be used as an alternative to he/him/his or she/her/hers. Usage of this particular set is becoming increasingly prevalent, particularly within the LGBTQ community.

Transgender: An umbrella term for people whose gender identity and/or gender expression differs from what is typically associated with the sex they were assigned at birth. People under the transgender umbrella may describe themselves using one or more of a wide variety of terms—including transgender. A transgender identity is not dependent upon physical appearance or medical procedures.

Transgender man: People who were assigned female at birth but identify and live as a man may use this term to describe themselves. They may shorten it to *trans man*. Some may also use *FTM*, an abbreviation for *female-to-male*. Some may prefer to simply be called *men*, without any modifier. It is best to ask which term a person prefers.

Transgender woman: People who were assigned male at birth but identify and live as a woman may use this term to describe themselves. They may shorten it to *trans woman*. Some may also use *MTF*, an abbreviation for *male-to-female*. Some may prefer to simply be called *female*, without any modifier.

Transition: Altering one's birth sex is not a one-step procedure; it is a complex process that occurs over a long period of time. Transition can include some or all of the following personal, medical, and legal steps: telling one's family, friends, and co-workers; using a different name and new pronouns; dressing differently; changing one's name and/or sex on legal documents; hormone therapy; and possibly (though not always) one or more types of surgery. The exact steps involved in transition vary from person to person.

Transsexual: Someone who has undergone, or wishes to undergo, gender affirmation surgery. This is an older term that originated in the medical and psychological communities. Although many transgender people do not identify as transsexual, some still prefer the term.

Further Reading & Internet Resources

BOOKS

Brown, John. *The Glass Closet: Why Coming Out Is Good Business.* New York: HarperBusiness, 2014.

The book offers inspiration and support for those who worry that coming out will hinder their chances of professional success.

Berry, Selise. *Out and Equal at Work: From Closet to Corner Office.* Out & Equal Workplace Advocates, 2013.

An anthology consisting of 36 stories from lesbian, gay, bisexual, and transgender business leaders who hold prestigious positions in the workplace, including those who work as executives at Fortune 500 companies.

Hall, David, M. *Allies at Work: Creating a Lesbian, Gay, Bisexual and Transgender Inclusive Work Environment.* Out & Equal Workplace Advocates, 2009.

A guide to creating cultural change in the workplace, developing work environments that fully include everyone regardless of their sexual orientation or gender identity/expression.

WEB SITES

genderspectrum. www.genderspectrum.org/groups/
A nonprofit providing resources and hosting online support groups for pre-teens, teens, parents, caregivers, and other family members.

GLAAD www.glaad.org
National advocacy and education organization dedicated to advancing human rights for LGBTQ individuals.

GLSEN. www.glsen.org
GLSEN (pronounced "glisten"), founded in 1990, is the leading national education organization focused on ensuring safe and affirming schools for LGBTQ students.

GSA Network. www.gsanetwork.org
An organization committed to fighting for educational justice by working with grassroots, youth-led groups and GSAs, empowering them to educate their schools and communities and advocate for just policies that protect LGBTQ youth from harassment and violence. Founded as the Gay-Straight Alliance Network in 1998, the group changed its name to Genders & Sexualities Alliance Network in 2016.

Human Rights Campaign. www.hrc.org
The largest national lesbian, gay, bisexual, transgender, and queer civil rights organization. With more than 3 million members and supporters nationwide, HRC envisions a world where LGBTQ people are ensured their basic equal rights and can be open, honest, and safe at home, at work, and in the community.

It Gets Better Project. www.itgetsbetter.org
The nonprofit It Gets Better Project, founded in 2010, exists to uplift, empower, and connect LGBTQ youth around the globe. The Project includes more than 50,000 video messages from people of all sexual orientations, including many celebrities, reassuring young people who face bullying and harassment that life does indeed get better.

PFLAG. www.pflag.org
The nation's largest LGBTQ family and ally organization. Committed to advancing equality through its mission of support, education, and advocacy, PFLAG has 400 chapters and 200,000 supporters in major urban centers, small cities, and rural areas in all 50 states, the District of Columbia, and Puerto Rico.

Lambda Legal. https://www.lambdalegal.org/
A legal resource for LGBTQ individuals who are struggling with discrimination based on their LGBTQ status. The organization provides a vast network of resources for you to research and in some cases can provide legal representation.

Index

Author's Biography

Melissa Albright-Jenkins has been a writer since she received her B.A. in English in 1994. She has written on a wide variety of topics, including those relevant to LGBTQ individuals. She lives in a progressive town and believes that all LGBTQ individuals should have equal access to the benefits and responsibilities that are offered to cisgendered individuals and straight people. Melissa has written one novel, *A Fork in the Road*, which deals with teenagers locked up in youth detention, and is working on a second novel as part of a mystery series featuring her departed friend Sara Noseworthy.

Credits

COVER

(clockwise from top left) iStock/AleksanderGeorgiev; iStock/kate_sept2004; iStock/TwilightShow; iStock/FluxFactory

INTERIOR

1, Shutterstock/Franco Lucato; 3, Shutterstock/Ben Gingell; 11, Dreamstime/Wavebreak Media LTD; 12, iStock/6okean; 14 (UP), Shutterstock/Gustavo Frazao; 14 (LO), Shutterstock/fizkes; 15, Shutterstock/atiger; 16, Shutterstock/Monkey Business images; 18, Shutterstock/Yulia Grigoryeva; 19, Shutterstock/Freature Flash Photo Agency; 20, iStock/Paul Bradbury; 21, Shutterstock/Kzenon; 23, Shutterstock/Memories Stocker; 24, Shutterstock/Pressmaster; 25, Shutterstock/Rawpixel.com; 26, Shutterstock/Rawpixel.com; 28, Shutterstock/Rawpixel.com; 29, iStock/Marco_Piunti; 30, Shutterstock/Rawpixel.com; 31, iStock/skynesher; 33, Dreamstime/Albert Shakirov; 34, Shutterstock/theskaman306; 35, Shutterstock/Glynnis jones; 36, Shutterstock/Gergely Zsolnai; 37 (UP), iStock/ferrantraite; 37 (LO), iStock/serefozdemir; 38, Shutterstock/Kaewmanee jiangsihui; 39, iStock/Tirthankar Das; 40, Dreamstime/Robert Kneschke; 42, Shutterstock/Rawpixel.com; 44, Shutterstock/Monkey Business Images; 45, iStock/DragonImages; 46, istock/AmberLaneRoberts; 47, iStock/FatCamera; 48, iStock/Tom Prout; 49, iStock/South_Agency; 51, iStock/LightFieldStudios; 52, iStock/asiseeit; 53, Shutterstock/GaudiLab; 54, Shutterstock/Whitney Lewiz Photography; 55, Dreamstime/Rawpixelimages; 56, Dreamstime/Monkey Business Images; 58, iStock/Ilsegagne; 60, iStock/NakoPhotography; 61, iStock/Fertnig; 62, iStock/Corners74; 63, Shutterstock/Standret; 65, iStock/Igusfrossi; 66, iStock/Sean Pavone; 67, iStock/Marco_Piunti; 68, Dreamstime/Wavebreak Media LTD; 69, Dreamstime/Wavebreak Media LTD; 70, Shutterstock/Kristi Blokhin; 71, Shutterstock/Blue Planet Studio; 72, iStock/FGTrade; 74, iStock/Andresr; 76, iStock/Twilight Show; 77, iStock/fstop123; 78, Dreamstime/Georgii Dolgykh; 79, iStock/fizkes; 80, iStock/asiseeit; 81, iStock/Steve Debenport; 83 (UP), Shutterstock/VGStockstudio; 83 (LO), iStock/NoSystem Images; 85, iStock/Anchly; 86, iStock/Weekend Images Inc.; 87, iStock/G-stock Studio; 88, iStock/FatCamera